KU-300-869

Man-eaters from the DEEP
and the not-so-deep

John Townsend

Published in association with The Basic Skills Agency

Hodder & Stoughton
A MEMBER OF THE HODDER HEADLINE GROUP

Acknowledgements
Cover: Blue Shark © Corbis

Photos: p. iv © Wild Country/Corbis, p. 4 © Paul A. Souders/Corbis, p. 9 © Stuart Westmorland/Corbis, p. 13 © Corbis, p. 22 © Ronald Grant Archive, p. 26 © Jim Zuckerman/Corbis.

Artwork: Brian Lee

Orders: please contact Bookpoint Ltd, 130 Milton Park, Abingdon, Oxon OX14 4SB. Telephone: (44) 01235 827720, Fax: (44) 01235 400454. Lines are open from 9.00 – 6.00, Monday to Saturday, with a 24 hour message answering service. Email address: orders@bookpoint.co.uk

British Library Cataloguing in Publication Data
A catalogue record for this title is available from The British Library

ISBN 0 340 84862 6

First published 2002
Impression number   10 9 8 7 6 5 4 3 2 1
Year   2007 2006 2005 2004 2003 2002

Copyright © 2002 John Townsend

Typeset by SX Composing DTP, Rayleigh, Essex.
Printed in Great Britain for Hodder & Stoughton Educational, a division of Hodder Headline Plc, 338 Euston Road, London NW1 3BH by The Bath Press Ltd, Bath.

Contents

The sea may look beautiful, but it has deadly creatures living beneath it.

1   Darkness Covered the Deep

So much of our planet is water. Dark water.
Often deadly.
It covers huge parts of the earth.
Over sixty per cent of the globe has water
more than a mile deep.
More people have been into space
than down into the deep dark sea.

There are shadows in rivers, lakes and seas
that we know very little about.
Some waters are so deep that no one
has been to the bottom of them.
No one knows what might live in the inky water
miles down in the cold.
Darkness still covers the deep.

But we do know about some of the things
that swim far down in the water.
Those that come up now and again and meet us.

Just below the surface there may be jaws
waiting to snap – ready to drag us down.

Since people first swam or set sail,
there have been stories of underwater killers.
We love to hear about them.
There is something deep inside all of us
that likes to shiver with fear
at what may be waiting just below the waves.

Today these water beasts are at risk.
We kill them in large numbers.
But now and again they remind us
that they need more respect.
They attack.
They might give us a nasty bite
or even eat us whole.
They may just leave us, of course –
floating face-down –
dead in the water . . .

2   Crocodiles

There are many stories and myths about crocodiles.
Yet there may be up to 1000 attacks
on people each year in Africa.
Nile Crocodiles can grow to over six metres long.
They lie just below the water in lakes,
rivers and swamps, waiting to strike.

A crocodile will grab its prey
and pull it down into the water.
It soon drowns the victim with its 'death roll'
before eating it in great gulps.
Any animal coming down to the water to drink
could become its prey.
Any person standing at the water's edge
could be a victim.

People who explored Africa in the last century
came back with some horror stories.

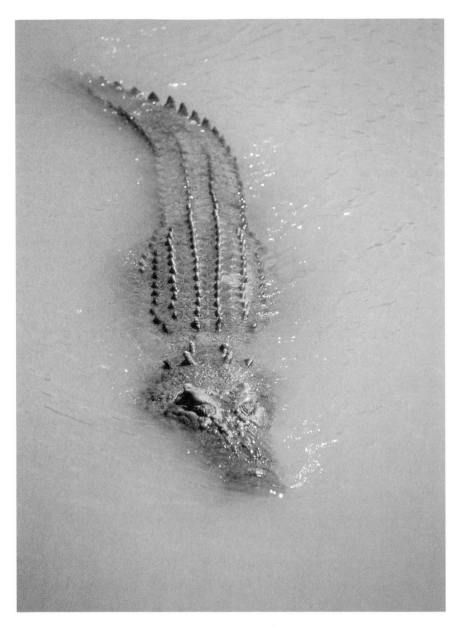

A crocodile lurking in the water, ready to snap up its next victim.

There were many more crocodiles then.
Reports of people being eaten alive were common.
People said one very large crocodile had
killed 400 humans!

One recent report tells of a crocodile attack
on the Congo River in Africa.
A man was out in the river in his small boat
when a crocodile's snout came through the water.
The man saw it and began to paddle quickly.
He got to a small island in the river.
He jumped out of his boat and ran up the beach.
But the crocodile did not give up.
It threw itself out of the water,
on to the sand bank, and ran after the man.
A group of tourists was watching
from a steamer boat.
They could only call to the man –
no one had a gun.

The man had nowhere to run.
He had to dodge past the crocodile
to get back to his boat.
The animal turned in a spray of mud.

With a quick swipe of its great tail,
the crocodile knocked the man to the ground.
Just as he was crawling to his feet,
it grabbed him in its jaws.
He screamed as it clamped his body
and shook him from side to side.
The crocodile dragged him down the beach
and plunged into the river.
They both went below the water
and were not seen again.

The people who had seen all of this happen
could only stand in horror.
There was nothing they could do.
It was just another attack by a creature
with a deadly record.

A hunter killed one such crocodile in 1968.
It was cut open and inside its stomach
he saw the remains of two goats,
half a donkey and part of a woman in a dress.
That's quite a dinner, even for a man-eater.

3   Sharks

Shout the word 'shark' in the swimming pool
and see what happens!
It's a word that many of us fear.
But very few sharks will harm us.
Even so, the sight of a fin cutting through the sea
will bring panic to any beach.

There are reports of shark attacks
on people each year.
Many have a happy ending.
Many bites are just from nosy sharks.
They take a quick bite to find out what's what!
Others may think we're seals or fish or turtles –
just another dinner.
Only a few will set out to hunt us.

Not all shark stories end in death.
A recent news story had a happy ending.

Dolphins Save Boy from Jaws of Shark

Dolphins saved the life of a teenage surfer by chasing off a 3-metre shark in New South Wales. Adam Maguire, 17, was surfing with friends when a shark bit him in the stomach. Suddenly a group of dolphins sped to the scene in a frenzy.

'All of a sudden they swam under us,' said Adam's friend, Brad. 'I looked over and saw Adam was knocked off his board. There was a hole in the board and a shark got hold of Adam. He was bashing at the water when the dolphins also joined in. They were trying to frighten the shark away.'

As the dolphins chased off the shark, the group of friends paddled to shore to raise the alarm. Adam was later taken to hospital. He was soon up and about again.

A dolphin expert later said, 'Dolphins often fight off sharks. In the wild this happens a lot when they feel under threat.'

It was lucky for Adam and his friends they were there to help.

Groups of dolphins such as these have been known to save
the lives of those being attacked by sharks.

Some of the worst shark stories
come from the days of war and shipwrecks.
When ships sank in warm seas,
sharks were soon on the scene.
As men clung to bits of wood in the water,
the sharks would home in – often in minutes.

Hundreds of pilots in World War II
were victims of sharks.
Many planes were shot down into the sea.
As men splashed in the water in their life-jackets,
the sharks moved in.
Even those in life-rafts told of sharks
that came to bite at the sides.
Many men lost feet or hands
to the jaws snapping round them.

When a fighter plane crashed
into the Pacific Ocean,
the two-man crew jumped into the sea.
All they could do was wait to be rescued.
They both wore life-jackets, which they
tied together to stop them drifting apart.
The sharks came in half an hour.
One of the men wore shorts
and he felt a bite at his foot.

The blood in the water brought five larger sharks.
The pilot hit out at each shark as it came past.
They left him alone but kept biting
at the man in shorts.
Suddenly both men were pulled underwater.
When the pilot came up again,
he saw the rope to the other life-jacket was cut.
The other man had gone.

For 16 hours the pilot had to wait for rescue.
The sharks kept brushing past him.
Once his face was hit by a flick from a large tail.
But at last rescue came.
Just in time.
Many other stories tell of sharks
that pick on just one person,
even though there are others to choose from.
Often it's those with bare legs
that get eaten first.

One tragic story comes from 1987
in the Sea of China.
A ferry was packed with people – far too many.
Late at night it hit a tanker containing petrol.
Fire ripped through the ferry.
The sea itself was ablaze.

The scene was total panic.
There was no time for people to get to life boats.
The only survivors were those who could
swim under water – below the flames.
Out of over 3000 people,
only two women and 23 men got out alive.
But there was another reason for this.

Large sharks (Great Whites, Tiger Sharks
and Blue Sharks) hunt at night
in the China Sea.
The noise, the smell, the splashing
and the blood brought swarms of sharks
to the wreck.
It was a rich feast for the hungry sharks.

The next day, the rescue boats did not
find a single body at the scene.
Sharks had beaten them to it.
Only 300 chewed-up bodies
were later found in the area.
Fishermen later found human remains
inside most of the sharks they caught.
No one will ever know how many died that night.
Those who didn't drown became the victims
of maybe hundreds of sharks.

The Great White Shark bites with three tonnes per square
centimetre in one snap of its jaws.

4   The Great White

After seeing the film *Jaws*, we all dread
meeting a great white!
It may be the main culprit for attacks on humans,
but this great fish gets a bad press.
Sadly, it is now under threat itself
in some parts of the world.
But is it really such a monster?

A large great white, 7 metres long,
is quite able to bite a human in two –
then swallow the pieces whole.
But it doesn't happen often.
When the shark senses a shape at the surface,
it will check it out.
After all, it could be food.
The best way for it to find out is to take a bite.
More often than not it will spit it out again.
After all, surf boards and wet suits
can't taste too good.

Not when the shark was hoping for a seal steak.

Each year a few people have a brush
with a great white shark.
Most escape. Some don't.
A recent attack happened at the end of 2000.

A newspaper headline said:
'CROWD IN CAFÉ SEES SWIMMER
KILLED BY SHARK.'
It told of an attack by a great white shark
off a beach in Perth, Australia.

Ken Crew was swimming about 30 metres out
from shore when the five-metre long shark
struck. People in a café saw it chase him as he
tried to reach the shore. It grabbed him in water
only 3 metres deep. A witness said, 'I heard yells
and screams so I looked down at the beach and
saw blood in the water.' The shark bit off the
man's leg. People got him on to the beach but he
died before help arrived.

Continued

Mr Crew's death was the third from shark attacks along this coast in 2000. There are about two deaths a year here from shark attacks. Even so, swimmers are 50 times more likely to die from drowning. Since 1791, more than 150 people have died from shark attacks on Australian beaches.

Great Whites tend to 'taste and spit'.
They take a bite just to see if they like it.
Humans don't make a good meal.
We're too bony and probably don't taste very nice.
Not like a juicy seal.
Their first bite is meant to
stop the victim fighting back.
If the shark doesn't like the taste, it will swim away.
Most people who die are not eaten.
They just bleed to death before help arrives.

It may not stop us dreading great whites,
but they often don't mean to hurt people.
One reason for this is that they
have their eyes shut when they bite.
Perhaps great whites aren't really so bad after all!

5   Giant Squid

Hardly anyone has ever seen a giant squid.
It lives in the deepest sea in the dark and cold.
It can be as long as two buses and weigh 2 tons.
It is said to have the largest eyes on earth -
as wide as half a metre.
Its mouth can cut through steel cable.
Its five pairs of long arms
can reach as far as 12 metres.
Each arm has large suckers on the end.
They grab fish, other squid and can even kill whales.
But do they eat us?

A story from 200 years ago tells of
the 'long arms of death' of a squid.
A Dutch ship was off the coast of West Africa
when the long arms of a squid came up out of the sea.
They pulled two sailors off the deck.
A third sailor grabbed a knife.
He cut the end of the squid's arm right off.
It was 15 metres long.

Perhaps this story is far-fetched.
Even so, it could be true.
It is just as well the Giant Squid
hardly ever comes to the surface.
When it does, we need to beware.

If you want to find out more about this
'monster of the sea', try this website:
www.giantsquid.org.

6   Killer Whales

Its name alone is scary.

So is its size.

This amazing beast can be 10 metres long.

It can also leap right out of the water.

It will even throw itself on to a beach to catch a seal.

But would it also grab a person

sitting by the shore?

Would it snatch you from your deck-chair?!

Do killer whales harm people?

True, they do kill a lot.

They eat seals, dolphins, squid, penguins

and anything that swims!

They often hunt in packs.

This way they can kill much bigger blue whales.

When fishermen once cut open a killer whale,

it had 32 full-grown seals inside!

Killer whales clearly keep on the look out for food.

The US Navy once warned
that killer whales always attack humans.
We now know better.
Even so, there are a few scary stories
about these great beasts.

It is unlikely that a killer whale
sets out to kill a person.
But, they might mistake a human for a seal.
They might even mistake a small boat
for another whale.
A number of stories tell of killer whales
that ram yachts.
Sometimes a killer whale has sunk a boat
or smashed it to pieces.

Killer whales are simply nosy.
They like to take a close look at humans.
Scuba divers often come up close
to nosy killer whales.
One diver was looking for lobsters
when he felt a tug on his foot.
A killer whale had his flipper in its mouth.
It then let go but swam all round him,
taking a good look.
It was even quite gentle.

Like their dolphin cousins,
killer whales are clever.
Many have been put in zoos for public shows.
Many have shown signs of stress at this.
Is it right to keep intelligent beasts
in small tanks to do tricks?
This is when some killer whales have hurt people.
Some have turned on their trainers.
Perhaps you can see why.

This is a true story:
People sat in their seats for the show.
The killer whale gave a great leap
and fell with a splash in its pool.
The front few rows were soaked. The crowd roared.
Next came the girl who waved and stood by the pool.
She smiled. She wore a pink swim suit.
There was a drum-roll as she jumped into the pool.
The whale swam round her.

She threw a fish and the whale
caught it in mid-air.
Now came the best part of the act.
This was where she rode bare-back
round the pool.

Do Killer Whales really live up to their name?

The whale swam under her
and she held on to its fin.
The crowd clapped as she sped round and round.
Suddenly the whale dived.
The girl went under. The crowd gasped.
There was a lot of splashing.
Then there was a scream. Blood.
The whale had the girl in its mouth.
It dragged her under. Men rushed to the pool.
They threw fish. They hit the sides of the pool.
The girl came up screaming one last time.
The whale pulled her to the bottom,
where she soon drowned.

A few other trainers have been hurt
by killer whales in zoos.
Sometimes the whales seem to go wild.
Is it cruel to keep these huge beasts
in such a small space?
After all, they like to swim for miles
in the open sea.
Killer whales are gentle giants of the deep.
Yes, they kill for food.
But it is rare for them to hurt us.

7   The Hippo

One of Africa's biggest human-killers is the hippo.
It can easily kill us under the water,
even if it won't eat us.
It doesn't eat meat.
But a hippo's jaws can bite a person in half.
And it will if you swim in its pool.
Hippos don't seem to like sharing!

A hippo's mouth can open to over one metre wide.
Its long teeth, like tusks, are similar to
the sharp prongs of a fork-lift truck.
If a hippo comes up under your boat,
you'll soon be in the water.
If it bites or pulls you under,
there's not much hope.
Bull hippos weighing four tonnes
have a lot of weight to throw around.
They kill people every year.

It was in 1996 when a safari guide
met a hippo in a bad mood.
A party of tourists was out in boats on the river.
They made sure they kept away
from a herd of hippos nearby.
But suddenly a large bull hippo
came up under the guide's boat.
There was a roar and a jet of spray.
The hippo's jaws were open wide
and the man fell into the huge mouth.

The teeth cut deep into his armpits
and his back.
The hippo dived, dragging the guide
down into the muddy river.
He was pinned face-down under the water.
It was pitch black.
Then the hippo opened its mouth.
The guide broke free and tried to swim away.
But just as he came up to reach the boat,
the hippo charged.
It grabbed the man from below.
Its teeth ripped through his foot
and pulled him under.
He knew the hippo could stay under for six minutes.

This Hippo could have you for breakfast – but would it want to eat you?

He could only last one minute at the most.
He kicked for all he was worth.
Once more the hippo let go.

Just as the man gasped for air,
it grabbed him a third time.
The jaws crushed his ribs.
In a rage, the hippo began dunking him
in and out of the river.
Blood sprayed into the water
as the teeth cut an artery.
All the man could do was
thump at the hippo's lips.

Suddenly the hippo spat him out and left him.
His arm was crushed and he'd lost a lot of blood.
One lung could be seen through
a big hole in his back.
They took him to hospital where
he needed a seven-hour operation.
It was touch and go.
He lost his arm, but at last the man pulled through.
He didn't go back on to that part of the river
for a long time to come.
Hardly surprising!

8   Water, Water Everywhere

All over the world,
hundreds of people drown each day.
Add to this all those killers that live in the water,
and you can see the scale of danger.
Without water we die. But with water we're at risk.

If we're not careful, even more of the earth
will be covered by water.
This is because the ice-caps are melting,
which means that the water is rising.

Will we meet these water beasts more often
as the floods rise?
Will it be them or us who ends up dead in the water?

Take care the next time you dip your toe in that water.
Just when you think it's safe to go back in there,
think again . . .
It may just bite back!